Becoming a Dentist in the U.S.

A Guide to Becoming A Dentist

Table of Contents

Introduction 3

Chapter 1: Overview of Dental Profession in the U.S. 4

Chapter 2: How to Become a Dentist in the U.S. 10

Chapter 3: Advantages and Disadvantages of being a Dentist in the U.S. 21

Conclusion 35

Introduction

I want to thank you and congratulate you for purchasing the book "Becoming a Dentist in the U.S.".

This book contains proven steps and strategies on how to become a dentist in the U.S.

Here's an inescapable fact: in order to stand amongst the other candidates, you need to start preparing yourself for this demanding profession. This book will help you understand and prepare you to embark on the journey of becoming a successful dentist.

If you do not learn the tips and tricks to help you prepare better, you may lose the opportunity to land your dream career as a dentist. Being a dentist is a challenging but an instantly gratifying profession because you get to help patients smile everyday. You can provide the best medical care to your patients and help them come out of severe toothaches or just give them a beautiful smile with your tools and precise motor skills.

Chapter 1: Overview of Dental Profession in the U.S.

The oral health of an individual is usually a reflection of his or her personal health as it is a good indicator of their overall dental hygiene, drinking and eating habits. The dental profession primarily deals with the treatment, care and maintenance of good oral health. It is one of the most sought after professions for various reasons attributed to the growing opportunities, respect within community, high compensation and rising demand for quality dental care.

In order to become a dental professional, one has to hold a degree in dentistry i.e., D.D.S. or D.M.D. degree from an accredited dental school. Once you complete the degree you have many career options, including:

- General or Specialist Dentist (self-employed, employee or partner)

- Federal Government (serve the U.S. armed forces as a Dentist)
- International Healthcare
- Academic (Teaching)
- Dental Public Policy
- Dental Research

The median pay for a dental professional in 2015 was approximately $158,000 per year, which translates to about $76 per hour. Dentists typically spend 36 hours per week in their practice, of which 33 hours per week is spent in providing treatment and care to patients. This allows a lot of flexibility with respect to number of hours they spend at work each week. Almost 80% of dental professionals are general practitioners while the remaining professionals are involved in some specialty practice like teaching, academic research, serving the U.S. armed forces or U.S. public services and serving international communities.

Dentists are generally trained to perform the following duties:

- Diagnose oral health condition of a patient using the latest tools and technology and provide appropriate treatment and care.
- Advice patients on oral health care based on evaluating their medical history, analyzing their diet, adopting effective brushing and flossing techniques and using the right teeth based products.
- Identify teeth and gum related issues and treat them through corrective surgery to improve appearance, speech, health and digestion. Also, diagnose and treat gingival and other tissues present in the oral cavity.
- Extract decayed or damaged tooth using effective procedures and replace them with implants, crown and other bridge techniques.
- Reduce pain and suffering induced during treatment procedures and surgery using effective anesthetic techniques and prescriptive medication.
- If you own a private practice then carve out some time to employ, supervise

staff, and oversee administration and day-to-day business operations.

Specialist dentists include:

- Orthodontics and Dentofacial Orthopedists – Diagnosis and treatment of abnormalities like irregular tooth development, missing tooth etc.
- Endodontists – Diagnosis and treatment of internal tooth issues related to dental nerves and pulp.
- Periodontists – Diagnosis and treatment of gum diseases and perform corrective surgery
- Prosthodontists - Extract decayed or damaged tooth and replace with implants, crown and other bridge techniques.
- Pediatric Dentists – Treat teeth related issues for children from birth till adolescence
- Oral and Maxillofacial Surgeons – Diagnosis and treatment of diseases, injuries and abnormalities related to the teeth.

- Oral and Maxillofacial Radiologists – Perform CT scan, MRI scan and imaging modalities of oral-facial structure, analyze results and report them.
- Oral and Maxillofacial Pathologists – Research and study cause and effects of all teeth related diseases.
- Dental Public Health Specialists – Instrumental in creating policies and developing programs like health care reform that could potentially affect our society.

There are inherent challenges as well as opportunities in the dental profession. Considering various factors like population explosion, changes within health care law, technological advance and a significant number of dentists from the 1960s and 1970s fast approaching retirement age, the dental profession definitely seems rewarding.

According to U.S News & World Report, Orthodontist and Dentist were ranked #1 and #2 respectively in "100 Best Jobs" list for 2016 and according to recent U.S. Bureau of Labor

Statistics; there will be an estimated 23,300 new dentist jobs created by the year 2022. The American Dental Association states that the practicing dentist-to-population ranges from 40-100 dentists per 100,000 people which is clearly low thus increasing demand for quality dental professionals to serve the ever growing needs of our community.

In summary, the benefits of being in the dental professional include:

- Serving the growing need of our community and shape the future of oral health care i.e. access to quality and effective oral care.
- Coming out of a dental school one can start his or her private practice and become independent and explore various career options within dentistry.
- Earn a handsome salary while maintaining a good work-life balance.

Chapter 2: How to Become a Dentist in the U.S.

Along with 8 years of focused study and good scores, you need to meet other requirements in order to become a dentist.

Meet the Pre-Requisites

First and foremost, evaluate yourself and decide whether this is the right profession for you. You need to be very skillful with your hands and also be a perfectionist, patient and posses good communication skills. You also need to display a high aptitude for Science. Most of the dental schools require mandatory completion of Bachelor's degree. It is recommended to take up Science major. You will have to take up all the courses that are a pre-requisite for the dental college you want to apply to. Make sure you go through their websites to find out the undergraduate course requirements. Most dental schools have similar requirements. For instance, in 2014 Baylor College of Dentistry required 6 hours of English, 8 hours of Organic Chemistry, 8 hours of Chemistry, 3 hours of Biochemistry, 14 hours of Biology, 8 hours of Physics, 3 hours of Statistics, etc. Typically your under graduation will take about 4 years to complete before you are eligible to apply to a dental school. To start with, take up physics, chemistry, biology and health in high school to prepare you for college. You can also take one 2D and 3D studio art class. You need to be highly dexterous with your hands if you want to succeed as a dentist. All these courses in college will help you to evaluate whether you have the acumen and interest to become a successful dentist, or not.

You can join dentist mentoring programs or the American Student Dental Association (ASDA). They support aspiring dentists and guide them through the dental school admission process. You can also participate in a dental school preparatory program. Robert Wood Johnson Foundation sponsors the Summer Medical and Dental Education Program (SMDEP). This program offers prospective dental students a six-week dental school preparation program at selected college or university campuses across the country.

They offer to students who are enrolled in their first two years of college. You can gain useful career development and financial advice. You can also find a first-hand view of dental work in a clinical setting.

If you want to start your own practice after graduation, you will require basic management skills and business acumen to help you manage and grow your practice. You need to be highly motivated and committed towards your career. Keep in mind that you may have to work for more than 60 hours every week initially to set up your practice and grow a good customer base. Marketing is essential if you want to practice in an urban area because you will surely face fierce competition from other dentists in that area.

Take the Dental Admission Test

Once you have completed your Bachelor's, you need to start preparing for the Dental Admission Test (DAT). Not only is your GPA score important for a good candidature, but also high scores in the Dental Admission Test (DAT) will better your chances to getting admitted in a dental school. To take the test, you need to pay a fee and schedule a date to take the test at a Prometric Test Center. You can also see the ADA (American Dental Association) website, http://www.ada.org/en/ for more information.

If you wish to learn more about becoming a dentist, you can go through professional associations like the American Dental Association (ADA) or the state dental associations.

The Admission Process

The admission process is the same for all the dental schools in the United States. All the dental schools will consider your Dental Admission Test (DAT) score, GPA, interviews and letters of recommendation during the admission process. Make sure you apply to the dental schools that are accredited by the

American Dental Association's Commission on Dental Accreditation.

The admission requirements are available on the college websites. For instance, the College of Dental Medicine at the Columbia University require the following:

- *A Bachelor's degree from a US accredited college or a Canadian institution is mandatory*
- *6 credits in English composition or literature or a writing intensive class in a non-English department (or the equivalent of one academic year of study)*
- *6 credits of Mathematics*
- *1 semester of Biochemistry*
- *A minimum of 8 credits (or the equivalent of one academic year of study), in the following subject areas (including lab):*
  1 year of Physics
  1 year of Biology
  1 year of Organic chemistry

1 year of Inorganic or general chemistry.

Once you meet the pre-requisites of a dental school, you will need to fill up the application for the dental school. You may need to pay a non-refundable application processing fee. Once you take the Dental Admission Test, you need to report your scores via AADSAS only. The colleges will not accept unofficial copies of your test scores.

You may also need to submit letters of recommendations from your college science professors, any dentist with whom you have volunteered, a mentor or researcher with whom you have worked, or one composite letter from pre-professional health advisory committee.

You will also need to submit college transcripts and other academic records as required by the dental college. Once you are selected you may need to appear for an interview with the admission committee of the dental college. You can also use the personal interview as an opportunity to ask anything about the dental school.

Attend the Dental School

Once you are accepted into a dental school of your choice, it is time to get serious about your career. You need to take all the courses that will benefit you later in your profession. Students taking the DMD and DDS programs take courses in topics like pathology, dental anatomy, physiology, oral microbiology, molecular biology, neuroscience, pharmacology, radiology and dental anesthesiology. Typically, during the first 2 years of dental school, you will focus on classroom and laboratory studies in health and dental science. You may take up courses like endodontics, pedodontics, periodontics, dental radiology, restorative dentistry, oral surgery, fixed prosthodontics, oral diagnosis, pediatric dentistry, removable prosthodontics, etc. The last 2 years of dental school will focus on real time experience with patients. You will have to diagnose and treat patients under the close watch of your superiors or dental instructors.

You can also gather professional experience in a dental office. You may consider part-time job if you can manage time effectively. It may not be possible to work for more than 10 hours per week. This will definitely provide you much more experience than you may get in your dental school.

Once you complete your courses in the dental school successfully, you will be awarded with a degree of Doctor of Dental Medicine (DMD) or Doctor of Dental Surgery (DDS). There is no difference between these two degree names.

Obtain License to Start Your Practice

If you want to practice, then you would require a state license. Requirements can vary by state but you will still need to pass the National Board Dental Examinations. This is a two-part written exam that will test your ethics, dental sciences and clinical procedures. Apart from this exam, you need to also pass the state's dental board exam. That state's licensing board approves these exams. Some states may also require prerequisites like CPR or first aid certification, an interview, a background check, etc. Some states host the exam annually or semiannually but laws may change frequently. It is recommended you check with the state's dental board for latest information about licensure requirements.

Choose a Specialization

Some dentists may want to just practice as general dental practitioners, whereas others like to continue their higher studies with a specialization. The different dental specialties that are recognized by the ADA's Council on Dental Education and Licensure are, Pediatric Dentistry, Dental Public Health, Endodontics, Oral and Maxillofacial Pathology, Oral and Periodontics and Prosthodontics.

To become a specialist you need to spend at least 2 to 4 years of additional education. You may additionally have to take a residency of up to 2 years before earning a specialty state license. You will face fierce competition for dental specialty programs. Only the very top candidates can earn a position in these programs. When you are in a dental school make sure you talk to the directors of the specialty programs so that you can prepare accordingly. Your directors will provide invaluable resources to you that can help you prepare for your continuing education.

Start Your Practice

Once you get your license, you can start your practice as a dentist. All you need to do is graduate from a dental school, pass your board exams and receive your license to practice dentistry. It may sound overwhelming but if you want to be a dentist you need to be patient, focused and highly motivated throughout your tenure of education. You can start your career by starting as an associate or partner in an existing practice, open your own private practice or even buy an existing private practice. Most dentists find opportunities through their school, or through career boards. You may also find positions through the network of professional contacts that you build throughout your dental school career.

If you are confident and want to open your own private practice, you will need to lease or purchase an office space, purchase the necessary equipment and supplies, and hire your dental assistants, receptionists, hygienists, etc. If you want to start a private practice, you may also need to work considerably more hours and accept appointments in the evenings and weekends to build a solid patient base.

You will also need to be licensed to prescribe drugs. This will require obtaining a state and federal license. You must also maintain and renew your state dental license. Make sure you remember to renew your federal and state drug licenses.

Chapter 3: Advantages and Disadvantages of being a Dentist in the U.S.

As a profession, you will find that being a Dentist is a very rewarding experience, although it can be challenging at times. Like many other professions, you will see pros and cons in this profession too. But the positives of being a dentist often overshadow the negatives of this profession. Dental schools can be expensive and tuition fees are increasing drastically. So you may not be able to clear the debt as early as you may estimate. Before you choose this profession, it is better if you go over the advantages and disadvantages of becoming a dentist.

Advantages of Becoming a Dentist

1. It is a highly respected profession

If you are a Dentist, you will be highly respected for sure. A dentist is trusted throughout a community. Patients will trust you to take care of them with your best ability and provide them the best medical care possible. Similar to other healthcare professions, dentists also hold a high status in their communities. A recent study from The Bureau of Labor Statistics has projected a 21% growth in the dental population from 2010 to 2020, due to this increased importance.

2. You will be helping people

When you are a dentist you will spend a lot of time helping people with their ailments. This will provide a lot of satisfaction and sense of accomplishment for you. This is a service-oriented profession so human interactions will happen every day. As a dentist you can bring smile to your patients, help them to love their teeth and improve their self-confidence sometimes. Helping your patients when they are in acute pain, and seeing the relief when you are done is something you can seldom find in any other profession. When you improve their smile or help them out of a pain, you will find instant gratification. You will definitely come home with a lot of good memories.

3. You will be in a stable profession

As a dentist you will be in an extremely stable profession. No matter how the economy is doing, people will need dentists as long as they continue to have teeth. So young or old, you will have patients always to cater to. Oral healthcare is critical to everyone, so you will have plenty of appointments to keep you busy. There is a need for cosmetic dentistry even more today because everyone wants to look beautiful, no matter what the age is. As long as you can make your patients smile, they will keep coming back to you.

4. Dentists have a good income

Dentists have a stable annual income of anywhere between $174,780 for a general practitioner to $322,200 for a specialist. So if you have the right business model, you can pretty much dictate how much you want to make. If you own a private practice, you can work according to your choice and make as much as you want. It is totally up to how hard you want to work.

5. You can balance your life

As a dentist, you have the flexibility to balance your personal and professional life. You can prioritize your family when you want depending on how much time you dedicate to your profession. If you own your private practice, this becomes easier. Since, you are not in a 9-to-5 job, you can choose how much you want to work every week. You will notice that most dentists work full-time but some may also work 3 days a week or even work just in the evenings or during the weekends.

6. You can be self-employed

As a dentist, you can start your own private practice whenever you wish. This gives you more freedom and flexibility. You can choose when to work. It is your own business, so make of it what you want to. Initially, most dentists start out as associates, but they eventually grow to become full partners. Sometimes they even open their own practices. You may even start out working for someone else, but if you confident and persistent, eventually you will be able to establish your own practice. This will give you the flexibility to make your own hours and your own decisions.

7. One of the Top 10 career choices

Dentistry is one of the Top 10 career choices in the United States. It has low unemployment rate, stable income and a flexible work-life balance. Everyone wants to maintain oral hygiene. So the demand for dentists will grow as the population grows. This means more people looking for dental care everyday.

8. Dentistry is still not covered by managed care

Amongst all the other healthcare professions, dentistry is the only one that is still not taken over by managed care. This means that as a dentist you can still enjoy some liberties and flexibilities if you manage your own practice. In future insurance companies may dictate a lot of the treatment that your patients can receive. In fact, government or insurance companies could be taking a more active role in managing dental care, so till then you can enjoy your private practice.

Disadvantages of Becoming a Dentist

1. **Education time can be long**

The time to complete your education to be become a dentist can take anywhere between 7-8 years after high school. You may have a requirement to complete Bachelor's degree to enter dental school. So typically you will spend your first four years of study at a university that will help you attain a Bachelor's degree. It is recommended you graduate with a Science major. Each dental school has different requirements so check with the ones you are interested to apply. You may need to attend specific classes that are required prior to entering dental school.

Once you finish your bachelor's from a University, you need to apply to a dental school. For that, you need to take the Dental Admission Test (DAT), appear for interviews and then finally get accepted. Typically, a dental program should take about 4 years to complete. You must know that it is a strenuous and challenging program. Once you graduate, you will receive a DMD or DDS degree. There is no difference between the two.

After you receive your degree, you can practice as a dentist. You can also continue with your studies. You can pursue Advanced Education in General Dentistry programs or a 1-year General Practice Residency if you like to gain more expertise and enhance your clinical skills as a general dentist. You can also specialize in one of the fields of dentistry that can take another additional 2-6 years, depending on the specialty you choose.

2. It takes time to establish yourself

Even after spending almost 8 years studying in a dental school, you will need to spend a lot of time in your profession before you create a customer base. It can be challenging and strenuous when you work full-time as a dentist. Sometimes you may have to stretch even on weekends and evenings. Since you are responsible for the oral healthcare of your customers, if you get an emergency call on Sunday night, you will have to attend it without any excuse. You have to find ways to give the best possible medical care to them. This may go beyond your usual business hours. Still in this profession you get to enjoy certain amount flexibility that you can use to your advantage.

3. **You will be in debt for sometime**

Studying in a dental college is not only time-consuming, but literally expensive. It is normal to hear a lot of dental students complaining about their debt. You will need around $250,000 to finish your education from a dental school. Some dental schools can be very expensive and that can incur you a debt of

$500,000 once your graduate. Once you graduate, you may spend on a house, a new car, etc. This way your debt will exponentially rise. If you want to start your own practice you may require $500,000 to start with. So, it can be a very expensive profession. Keep all this in mind when you are applying for dentistry.

4. There is stress associated with this profession

Being a dentist is not easy. It can be very exhausting and stressful. There will be fierce competition between dentists and also you will have the looming debt over you. Sometimes you will have to even manage people or staff in your private practice. When you have tough patients or problems, it will also add on to your daily stress. Sometimes you may have to work on a confined area for a few hours. You will be handling all types of patients, some who are terrified by dentists and the tools they use. There may be plenty of reasons you may encounter that can cause stress to you. You should be able to cope with this stress and also manage it well so that it doesn't affect your health.

5. It can be physically challenging sometimes

Working as a dentist can be difficult and physically challenging at times. You may also encounter neck pain. Since you are bound on confined areas for longer time, you may encounter issues with your neck, back, hands and shoulder. Dentists are usually susceptible to hypertension, chronic back problems, Carpal tunnel syndrome, etc. If you don't take care of yourself from the beginning, you will have to visit a chiropractor pretty soon.

6. You may be susceptible to infectious diseases

Since you will be treating patients every day, you are more susceptible to infections or contagious disease. You will always be at a risk of contracting a blood borne disease such as Hepatitis C or HIV, if the patient is a carrier. Apart from these, you can contract common infections, such as flu, etc. Even though chances are very low, nevertheless, you need to be careful while working with your patients.

7. **You may have little free time for yourself**

It is quite normal to have very little free time for yourself when you are a dentist. It may not always be feasible to go on long vacations without being disturbed at any time. If it is your own practice, then you will have to continue to pay your staff even when you are away and not working yourself. This means added expenses when income is zero at that time. So you cannot take a vacation for more than two weeks, otherwise your vacation will cost you a lot.

8. **Dentistry has one of the highest suicide rates amongst any profession**

Statistics claim that dentists tend to have the highest suicide rate. It is common since they are under continuous stress and grieving patients, along with long hours of work. Debt can also be overwhelming. It can be physically demanding and also emotionally challenging. All these factors may attribute to a higher suicide rate among dentists.

9. You will face fierce competition in this profession

You can face sever competition when applying to dental schools as more and more students are applying each year. Since dentistry is the only area in the healthcare industry that has not been taken over by managed care, more students want to get into this profession. The flexibility and freedom associated with this profession is immense. If you need to get into a good dental school, you need to maintain high GPA and high DAT score.

Even after you start practicing, you will still find competition among your fellow dentists. If you want to practice in an urban area, make sure you do some serious marketing to attract a good customer base.

10. You don't get any benefits in this profession

As a dentist you may not go on long vacations when you have to pay for the expenses managing your private practice. There will be daily expenses even when you are not there. Also, you wont get any benefits like other jobs. You will have to invest wisely and make sure you have all the required insurances so that you can retire in peace when you want.

11. You will need Business Management skills

If you want to start your own practice, you will need to run it like any other business. You will essentially be a business owner, an entrepreneur and also the main employee providing the dental services. You need to manage your staff well. You need to know how to keep them happy, financially and otherwise. You may need to handle different types of employees. It may be frustrating and stressful at times. You need to hone people management skills too. As a dentist, you have to learn to juggle between multiple roles. This is something you cannot learn at any dental school.

Everyone has an idea about how his or her career will be like. No career is perfect or the way you want it to be. There will be advantages and disadvantages that you have to live with. Just make sure you understand the drawbacks that will tag along with this profession and also the immense joy you will receive helping others smile.

Conclusion

Thank you again for purchasing this book!

I truly hope this book helped you understand how to become a dentist in the U.S.

Your next step is to evaluate if this is your career choice. If yes, then start moving in the right direction. Start with the pre-requisites, then prepare for the Dental Admission Test (DAT) and finally apply to a dental school. Once you graduate, you can choose to specialize or start practicing as a general dental practitioner.

Click here to leave a review for this book on Amazon!

Thank you and good luck!

Made in the USA
Middletown, DE
20 December 2018